"FILLED WITH INS[...]
AN INTENS[...]"

THE BATTLE WITH THE
SUBCONSCIOUS MIND

A JOURNEY OF HOW I CHANGED THE WAY I THINK SO I CAN BECOME THE MAN I WANT TO BE.

The Battle with the
SUBCONSCIOUS MIND

LEONARD "NOSTRA" DENIS

© Nostra's Word Publishing

I would like to express my deepest appreciation to all those who provided me the possibility to complete this book . God is always number one then my sister Geraldine. A special shoutout I give to My friend Earlson Satine, whose contribution in stimulating suggestions and encouragement,
  helped me to coordinate my project especially in writing this book.
   Furthermore I would also like to acknowledge with much appreciation the crucial role of people like, Nicole Benns, iJanice C, Davis , Nawaal Anderson, Sabrina Riley, Rik Lennon and Greg Sampson who   help me to stay on task! Last but not least, many thanks go to the My Parents siblings and my kids who have invested their full effort in guiding me in achieving my goal. I appreciate the guidance given by them as well as my haters especially that don't want me to win... this is book 3 LETS GO!

My Thoughts 3

People will throw stones at you.
Don't throw it back. Collect them all
and build an empire

PROLOGUE

For some time now, I set out on a journey to find my success. This journey was not an easy one. I failed many times. I was mocked, ridiculed and made fun of through this entire journey. Yet still, with all the roller coaster of emotions. I learned a lot along the way. The main purpose of this book is to train you for the difficulties that you will face in your journey towards success. I have learned all these things the hard way and I don't want the same to happen to you. I used to work a regular job. I didn't like the job but never showed any effort in leaving, I had a lot of dreams of working for myself but never bothered to take action. It was only after getting fired that I realized I had to do something now. It was a now or never situation for me. I was lost for some time but eventually I found my purpose. I learned from many people and trusting the process even when my mind told me to give up. This book is about my journey of changing the way I think so that I become a man that I wanted to be.

when things didn't come easy to me. I worked much harder. After many failures, I kept consistent in my efforts. My persistence helped me find likeminded people who mentored me and helped me find my own way. I've discussed everything from start to the end. I want you to work for your own self instead of working for someone else. When you decide to work for yourself, things don't come easy to you. You have to earn everything by working your ass off and the results of all the hard work is worth experiencing. After reading this, I hope you get a greater appreciation of how the mind works , and how changing your thoughts makes yourself eligible for success that doesn't come to everyone. It only comes to those who try to find it.

CHAPTER 1

ACCEPTING BEING BASIC

❖

Oftentimes we hear the word mediocre without understanding its true meanings. From childhood to manhood, most of us believe that being a mediocre person will get us through life. Being a mediocre is thought as being normal. At least you are not a failure. You are just good enough to live your life. But what does it mean to be a mediocre? Being an average person with an average mind and an average thinking and work ethic, right?

Your performance is never too bad and never too good. You are just an average person and are successful in the eyes of the people around you. They praise you for your good enough grades, your good enough job, your good enough house, your good enough car and your good enough… This praise makes you think that being a mediocre is being normal and you can continue to be like the way you are. You don't need to work harder to achieve more because you've got all what's needed to live a life. You are good with being a mediocre person who has a good balance in life.

In actual, being a mediocre doesn't mean that you're normal. People might praise you for your accomplishments but you're still not normal. You can only be a mediocre when you are not working up to the fullest of your abilities. You have the ability to achieve more but you settle for less. And that's because this less is enough for you and you don't need more. Or you just think that you don't need more because who doesn't?

Here is where the battle with your subconscious mind starts. Instead of settling for the mediocrity and accepting it as your fate, you need to settle this mediocrity itself and work against it. You can achieve much more by putting in a bit more work than you are putting in right now. A small amount of effort can bring about a big change. If you multiply 1 by itself for 365 times, i.e. the number of days in a year, you get 1 as the answer. And now look at this! If you multiply 1.01 with itself for 365 times, what do you get? Beyond your imagination, the answer is 37.78. Yes, that's what you get. What's the difference between 1 and 1.01? It's so small that we often ignore it while doing maths. But in real life, it makes a huge difference. Imagine making small progress everyday. What you can achieve after a year is beyond your imagination. The only thing you need is a little extra effort and consistency because consistency is the key to success. Without being consistent you can never achieve any goal you set. Stopping rusts your abilities. It makes you even weaker than before. My purpose here is to teach you from self experience. I can share my knowledge but it's your duty to actually start working and putting in some effort before you can taste the results. I can share with you precise and tested ways to avoid being a mediocre and settle the mediocrity, once and forever! Let's do it.

First thing to do is to evaluate where you stand. Look around yourself and compare yourself to others. People who are behind you and people who are ahead. Think and know your place. Be grateful when you see people who are behind you and be motivated by the people ahead of you. Have you ever looked at results of economical surveys? The surveys which tell you about the average American's financial situations. These surveys should be a source of motivation for you. Look at where the average American stands and compare yourself to them. Being an average means being a mediocre and you don't want to be a mediocre, right?

After you have made a good evaluation of your position in your community and in your country, you need to have goals and a plan to achieve those goals. If you ever want to get out of a situation, you always need to have a goal and a plan. Mediocrity is actually a situation and you can come out of this situation by continuous hard word and persistence. Goals make it easier for you as they become your motivation. The bottom line is to have a goal. Without a goal, you'll be lost. You won't be able to stay strong for a long time because you won't have any motivation. Stop here for a few minutes and think about things you really want to achieve in your life. Did you stop or have continued reading? If not, I request you again. The time is now to think about it!

Once you have set a goal, or a multiple goals, then you need a plan to achieve those goals. Plans are like paths. A good plan is like a smooth road without much bumps but still many uphills and downhills. A bad plan is like a road with many potholes in addition to the uphills and downhills. But the thing is that you ultimately reach your destination i.e. you goal. That is what matters the most.

If you have invested a good amount of time in making your plan and have taken in account your circumstances and limitations, it's definitely going to be a good plan. But remember that you only slow down a bit on curves and uphills on a road but you never stop. Same goes for a plan. You will slow down at times but all you need to have is the fire in the belly and you are good to go. You can go miles and won't get tired. That's what a goal and a motivation does for you. That is why setting goals is not only necessary but also very helpful. And it should not be a random thing, it should be a thing you can not live without. If you have a desire so strong for something, you are actually blessed. That desire has now become your goal and your motivation.

Intact it's a mind game. Once you have made this thing clear to your mind that you are never going to sit back and just let things be, you would have a new energy to do things you never wanted to do before. You will find it easier to stick to a routine and turn it into your success. Setting a routine is important in order to bring consistency in your life.

Your daily timetable should be divided into hours. You should have tasks allowed to each part of your day so that you don't spend free time without working on anything beneficial. Keep rest hours a part of your schedule. Reload in these hours in order to stay focused and efficient in your work hours. Except for the rest hours, you should always be busy doing something productive. When you try to keep yourself busy, it will be easier for you to try something new. Whenever you try something new, you learn many things from it. Some things even help you in other chores which you have been doing for years but never realized that you were lacking something. Trying new things will also give you confidence that you can do things you have never done before. This confidence can be translated into taking bigger risks which can transform your life completely for the better.

Until now, it must be clear to you that being a mediocre is not a natural thing and it's not normal. It is indeed the absence of hard work. You were not being you until now. Now is the time to start being you and transform your life. As I said earlier, instead of settling for the mediocrity, you need to settle this mediocrity itself. Settling of mediocrity is a major initiative you must be willing to take in order to start working towards a better future which you definitely deserve. And why won't you? Everyone deserves a better future. The only need of the hour is hard work, persistence and fire in the belly. The time is now!

CHAPTER 2

THE NAPOLEON HILL EFFECTIVELY

❖

I consider a self-help book like this to be incomplete without mentioning the man who turned impossible into possible. Born into poverty in rural Virginia in late 19th century, this genius went on to become rich beyond imagination. Napoleon Hill was no ordinary man but a truly gifted genius who turned his life around and never accepted to settle for less. He never thought of conditions he was born into as normal and strived for greatness and with hard work and persistence, he not only reached his goals but had success beyond his own imagination. The thing which made him even more famous is his book "Think and Grow Rich", a bestseller published in 1937. It is an inspiration to millions and millions of people. He has indeed done a great favor to us by writing this book.

Many of us believe that this book was the end result of his career since it made him famous and is one of his most successful ventures. The truth is that he experienced a lot of failures before being able to give advice to others. He started businesses which resulted in his bankruptcy but it never stopped him from working. He tried and tried again until he became the man we all know. The Napoleon Hill we don't know was a complete failure. It's ironic that people only get famous when they get rich and we get to see their success only. Before assessing his success, it is necessary to have a look at his failures, because failures are what make you strong and give you experience.

He shares the most basic principle of becoming rich in his book and that's thinking of becoming rich. As I mentioned earlier, it's a mind game. Once you have trained your mind to think the way rich people think, half the job is done. When you have got that state of mind, you will attract the people who are already rich. It would become much easier for you to learn from mistakes that they committed in their past. This is not only limited to mistakes but future plans too. The plan which you must devise should have some input from the experienced. You attract what you become conscious of. When you become failure conscious, you attract failure. If you choose to think more positively, you will attract success. You see, it's more about what you expect. It's like your mind sends signals to the universe and whatever the signal is, the returned signal is just the same. Positive mindset does a lot for you. It not only gives you confidence but also makes you stand out from a crowd and makes other people give you the attention you deserve.

When you think about something constantly, it eventually becomes your desire. It helps you choose your goals more wisely. When money is your target, your goals will be centred around it. You will choose a business that you think will bring the most amount of money. It's all about the consciousness of your mind. Or more about the subconscious of your mind. It affects your day to day work without letting you notice it. You keep making small progress without noticing and when you have reached your goal, it's only then that you realize what was driving you through all this time. But in order to reach that state of mind, first thing you need to do is train your mind to always think like a rich man thinks. Because that mindset is what's going to get you through all the failures and difficulties you meet on your path. It is worth noting here that being rich doesn't mean money rich only. It means having lots of everything including health, happiness and business success.

Thoughts become things is a reality. Have you ever felt better right after visiting a doctor who assured you of getting better by using the prescribed medication? What makes that happen? It's your thoughts and your subconscious. Without knowing, you make yourself feel better by just thinking of being healthy. That is how it works with other things. When you think of yourself to be successful, you actually become successful. But it is way easier said than done. When you are in a tough situation where you are not getting the desired results and things are not going your way, it becomes more and more difficult to think positively, let alone thinking about success. And that's what separates successful people from the unsuccessful ones. It's not going to happen overnight that you suddenly start thinking about everything positively. It will happen gradually because bigger changes come about gradually and then they stay for a long period of time. You have to change your mindset and that will take time so patience is the key. Brain train yourself. Practice your positive thinking ability everyday and in every task you perform. Once you have achieved this state of mind where you see the positive things in a bad situation, your time has arrived and your training is done. Now you can see the results. Again, patience is the key!

Taking control of your thoughts is a feat to accomplish. The big question here is how to take control of your thoughts. It's not possible to do it by just saying it or reading it or listening to it over and over again. You need to have a burning desire for something. A desire that takes over your mind and becomes your motivation. Something you really want to achieve. It can be a car, a house, a relationship, or anything for that matter. As long as it makes you crazy, it's a good fuel for your success. The most important thing here is that the desire should not be vague but definite. You should not be running for something you can't actually understand. It should be a specific thing which can take over your mind. Vague desires would only make you tired and won't let you achieve anything. A specific desire will help you set a specific goal. You can start working on it from day one! It will make you think about itself and when you think about one specific desire and think that you are going to achieve it, what are you actually doing? You are actually training your mind to think positive. That's what your desire does for you.

When you desire for something and love it so much, you never want to not achieve it. You always think about achieving it. Your mind doesn't let you think about not achieving it. And that state of mind is what you need to be successful. Because your thoughts become your destiny. When you want something, you actually send signals to the universe and the universe sends back signals of its own and the thing you want starts getting attracted towards you and that is how you achieve it. Go back to where you have to start. It's the positive thoughts of being able to get what you want and for that you need a definite desire. So first things first, think about what you desire the most. Something you can't live without. Once you have it in your mind, now you need to have faith that you are going to achieve it. The faith in being successful makes you successful. If you don't have faith in yourself, everything would seem impossible. Having faith gives you the strength to keep going. Having faith during critical and difficult situations is not easy but you can do it. The simple way to do it is to tell yourself again and again that you can achieve what you are working for. Reaffirmations make you have faith. It's called playing with your subconscious. You trick your mind into having faith in yourself. The way to do it to tell yourself repeatedly. There's no other way you can have faith in yourself when a difficult situation arrives. Say it loud and say it repeatedly that "All will be well."

CHAPTER 3

BATTLE OF THE MIND

❖

    Until now, I've been stressing on the battle of the mind while talking about other things. I feel like it's time to share something personal to let you know what I have been through. I had one job for 18 years. And this one job was my whole world. I started working at this nursing home when I was still in school. I went to college and graduated while keeping this job. I put my sweat and blood into this job and worked hard to earn what I was earning. It's a natural thing that when you are achieving more than others, you definitely get noticed. I also got noticed but for all the wrong reasons. The management started to dislike me instead of liking me for my efforts to encourage others to be great .they didn't like it that I was a leader and really didn't need them to make a difference . What they didn't realize was even though the had authority more than I , I was putting in the effort they were not putting in. Their dislike for me resulted in me getting fired from the job. My world came down suddenly. This job was an essential part of my life. I was so used to this job that I didn't know what to do after losing it. I never saw it coming since my performance was much better than my peers. On my part, the mistake that I had committed was that I put all my eggs in one basket. I didn't have another stream of income. I was totally dependent on this job. All of this made me realize the gravest mistake I was committing through all these years. I felt normal working that job and had thought about retiring with the same job. But things don't always go our way especially when we are not ready for a curve ball. It was a test of my nerve and I'm proud to say it that I made it through all of this. But it was not as easy as I just said it. It took me two years to stand back on my feet and say to the world that I exist.

The reason I was able to do all of this and get back on my own feet is that I won the battle with my own mind. In the beginning, I put the blame on others. I put the blame on the management for being jealous with me and firing me I even wrote a song about the manager that fired me. Soon I realized that it won't do any good for me. I had to live with the fact that I got fired from a job that I served for 18 years. I realized that we are all replaceable.

My purpose here is to teach you the importance of realizing the battle of your own mind. Most of us don't even realize that the greatest battle is actually going on in our own minds. The battle between the negative and the positive thoughts. The battle between success conscious and failure conscious. It is us who control these battles and still we don't know about these battles. The first step is to realize that there is a battle going on, the next step is to help the positive thoughts and your success conscious win this battle.

I've been emphasizing over this for some time now. The battle can only be won by staying strong and by keeping yourself on the right path. You need to keep yourself away from things which confuse you. You need to have a strong will in order to win this battle.

This battle is just like any other battle which is fought between two or more groups of people. Have you ever seen a weaker group win a battle? Sometimes one group seems strong by it's bigger number but it's not always strong. The numbers don't always matter. It's the strength of the individuals in the groups that matters. When you train your brain to become tough and to live through all the difficulties, it's only then that you can win this battle.

Negative thoughts plague your mind. Their only purpose is to give you a set back and not let you stand on your feet. They can be very harmful if not controlled. The irony is that it's you and only you who can fight against them. That is because you own your mind and you should be able to do what you want to do with it.

There are certain things which make you think negatively.

If you worry about things too much, the worry will take over your mind and make you feel like you can't achieve things you want to achieve. Worries fill your mind with negativity. They take up a lot of space in your mind and don't let you think about the positive aspects of trying something new. The way to not get trapped by worries is to talk to yourself and give yourself reaffirmations that you are going to get what you want no matter what. When you stop caring too much, you stop worrying about little things. They don't matter to you anymore. It doesn't matter what's the result, your mind pushes you to do everything your way once you stop worrying.

Fear is a lethal killer. It can kill your dreams like no other thing can. It doesn't let you take even a single step. It makes your body paralyzed. The fear of failure is the biggest hurdle in your path towards success. Many people would be successful today had they not gotten over by this fear of failure. This fear has it's roots in 'what people would say'. The first thing to do in order to get this fear out of your mind is to make a deal with yourself. To stop worrying about what people would say. It's definitely not easy because we have to live with these people after all. And we have to face them each day. Most of them are happy when we are unsuccessful because it is how it is. It takes a lot of courage to face people when you are not successful yet. They call you crazy and all those things which you don't want to hear. They mock you for taking that stupid step of not following the trend and choosing your own way. They make you remember that they warned you that you were going to fail. It's not easy to face people but you have to face them with one and only thing in your mind. That a day will come when these same people will praise you for your bold decisions. The decisions that helped you achieve what they couldn't.

    But before that, you have to convince yourself that you will be successful. Because you can only attract success by being success conscious. And for that you have to start thinking positively. Think like you have achieved your goals and you will achieve them one day. Because remember, your thoughts become your destiny. Whatever you are trying to find is also finding you. If it's success then it will come running towards you. The only challenge is to not let your fears take over the battle which is going on in your mind. It's you who has the power to take over the battle and you should take over it.

When you are down and out, you are vulnerable to depression which eats your brain like rust eats iron. We all know how strong iron is but it's weak when comes in contact with rust. Same goes for your mind. You should understand how strong it is. But if you let it contact depression, it won't stay strong for long. Again the same thing, brain train your mind to avoid all the negativity. Fill your mind with positivity. Always think like you have achieved success already and it is a matter of time that you will see yourself be successful. Remember that being successful is not the actual success, but thinking of being successful during times of distress is. And that's because when you think about success, you actually become successful. It's a complete circle.

Coming back to my story, I have two successful businesses running as of now. The reason I was able to get out of that difficult time is that I won the battle of my own mind. You can do that too but it takes patience and persistence.

CHAPTER 4

MOTIVATION VS WILL

❖

Most of the time, we think of motivation and will as two same things. In fact, they are much different than each other. In simple words, motivation is the reason to do something while will is the energy that you must possess to do that thing. They both are very much interconnected and can not be separated. In order to achieve your goals, you don't only need motivation but also the willpower to start doing it and then to stay strong while you keep doing it.

It's not easy to be motivated. You only need a desire to motivate yourself. And desires come naturally to us depending on our interests. If you desire of getting rich, you will be motivated to start a business and work tirelessly on it. But that motivation alone is never enough. It needs to be supported by a strong energy which you must possess. And that energy is your willpower. It is what gets you up early in the morning when others sleep. It helps you work late hours when others stop working. It keeps you going. It's more related to your self-control. How much can you push yourself towards doing something even if you lack motivation. If you have decided to start doing something, how far you go is decided by your willpower.

If you possess a strong willpower, things tend to get much easier for you. A weaker willpower gets dominated by fears and negative thoughts. In order to be able to achieve something, you must have the will to achieve it. You must have that energy, that fire in the belly to go an extra mile to get what you want to get. What a physically strong man can do, a weak man can't. Your willpower is your mental strength just like your physical strength. When you are weak, you train your body, get physically fit and are able to do what you couldn't do before. Same goes for your brain. If your willpower is not strong enough to push you through the most difficult of situations, all you nees to do is train your brain. Make it fit for the difficult situations. Give this training some regular time, just like you would go to a gym regularly in order to get physically fit. When you make something your habit, you actually reduce the chances of yourself getting fatigued. Just like that, when you train your willpower daily, there are reduced chances of it getting fatigued and wearing out.

Your motivation is just your fuel while your willpower is your engine which actually propels you towards success.

Writing this book was a challenge for me before I started doing it. Once I had the courage and the will to start it, now it seems achievable. I had my motivations before starting it and I still have them. But to actually start doing it needs willpower and I took my time building my willpower. It took me days to adjust to the thought of writing a book like this. Once I was done with this, it seems much easier now. I always felt like I could do it, and now it seems possible. Because your thoughts become your destiny.

Willpower is not always about starting to do something. Sometimes it's about stopping something not beneficial for you if you want to achieve those goals. Any bad habit which comes in the way of your goals must be abandoned. It's about controlling yourself when you don't want to be controlled. If you are successful in controlling your own self, you have achieved half of your success already. Because this one ability is so rare in this world that only a few can master it.

Taking control of your thoughts also helps you build up your willpower. When you think positively about doing something, you are more likely to do that thing. Your mind gives you all the reasons to do that because it's only looking at the positive aspects.

You must be familiar with the famous Nike phrase, "Just do it". It's not famous for no reason but because it has made many people achieve their goals. When you think about just doing it, you simply go for it without thinking for a second time. You have the mindset and willpower it takes to go for it. While you must understand that setting a goal and making a plan is necessary to achieve something, it's the mental strength that is required to take a sudden action that makes you start doing it. If you continue to think, think and think, your mind is more likely to get filled with worries and doubts. These worries and doubts when combine with fear of failure, make it impossible for you to achieve your goals. The bottom line here is that you must possess the willpower and mental strength to go for it at the first instance. Otherwise it gets much difficult as you give more time to thinking about whether to do it or not.

While emphasizing too much on the willpower, you must not forget the importance of motivation. Motivation brings the idea of doing anything. Without motivation, you don't even know what to do. And that's because it's driven by the burning desire inside of you. The desire which you have for many many years but have never bothered to think about it because of your fears. The desire becomes your motivation. Once you have a motivation, then you need a strong willpower to work for it.

An engine can do nothing without fuel and the fuel has no importance if you don't have an engine.

Researches show that 92% of the people never get to accomplish their new year's resolutions. They have the motivation to do something but lack the willpower to actually do it. There is a huge difference between wanting to do something and doing it actually. Motivation only gives you a dream. It's your willpower that makes you turn that dream into reality. A dream without a willpower to achieve it always remains a dream.

Willpower is your inner strength that helps you overcome fear, worries and other obstacles you might face on your path towards success. It is your strength which decides how far you can go. Many people have a certain limit of it and hence lose hope after some time. They can't take the grind anymore and stop working towards their goals. While the ones who go on to become successful show persistence. They do so because they possess the level of willpower required to pursue their dreams. They are always ready to face uncomfortable situations that they never faced before. It is a natural thing that if you stick to a plan, keep executing it over and over again with little improvements, you finally achieve what you want to achieve. It's just a matter of time and patience. And that is the most difficult part of every journey towards success. It requires time and patience which most of the people lack.

I can not over emphasize the importance of willpower. It gives you the courage to face whatever hurdles come in your way. It gives you the strength to face difficult circumstances while keeping your cool. It gives you the ability to reject any sort of temptations and helps you visualize the bigger prize which awaits you. It helps you get back on your feet after a set back. Achieving your goals is in your own hands. The only thing that matters is how willing are you.

CHAPTER 5

PROCRASTINATION IS LIKE MASTURBATION

❖

Procrastination is the worst of all things that exist on this Earth. This thing has destroyed peoples' lives like no other thing has. I believe that it is a disease which infects your mind and makes it unable to work. I know it's not a nation, never mind that but it's so dangerous that I had to make this comparison. I can talk all day about it but the point I want to make here is how procrastination makes you unable to achieve your goals.

It is basically a challenge that we all face before doing anything we need to do. Our minds tend to think about all the not so important chores and distract us from our work. Procrastination essentially means to delay things but you can't delay things by just sitting back. You get involved in other activities while knowing that you shouldn't be wasting your time there and should work on something more beneficial. It's like a force but a negative one that pushes you away from your tasks.

My goal here is to break down the reasons of procrastination and finally come up with a solution so that you can stop yourself from falling into this trap and can achieve what you want to achieve.

You must have heard this quote that goes like 'Procrastination is like masturbation, in the beginning it seems good but after some time you realize that you are only screwing yourself'. I completely agree with it since it's the truth. You enjoy yourself while procrastinating but later regret when you face the results of it. It makes you lazy and you can't concentrate on anything. You just want to get away from anything which requires even a little bit of effort. It eats you from the inside without you noticing.

Procrastination never gives you pleasure over long term. Instead it gives you regrets. You are unable to perform even the smallest tasks if you have been a procrastinator all your life. You always find a way to get away from the tasks which you need to perform. You always have an excuse or something else to do but not the actual task. It takes a hit on your self esteem while also damaging your willpower and your motivation has no importance all of a sudden.

In order to understand why we procrastinate, we need to know about our psychology first. Everything we do is governed by our psyche. It is basically our mindset that makes us do all the things that we do. You see the roots of it now? It's again connected to your thoughts. The basis of procrastination is the fear which we have before we start doing something. Sometimes we are not familiar with a task and are doing it for the first time. The fear of trying something new is real. Since you haven't been through a similar situation before, you don't know the ups and downs you would face and hence keep delaying the task day by day. Eventually it becomes a habit and you end up delaying every other task which needs to be done on time in order to be beneficial for you. Your college or office reports matter nothing once the deadline or the meeting is over.

We tend to be attracted towards things which give us instant results. Why do you think people waste their money in lotteries and bets? It's the instant prize that makes them do so. The same people would never invest a $100 in a growing company but waste hundreds of dollars at the bar. It's because they are after the instant pleasure and happiness. The idea of getting everything instantly is based in our greed for everything. We are not only greedy for money but for everything including happiness, pleasure, relaxation and the list goes on. We want instant results and we are so used to this thought of getting an instant prize that we eventually stop caring about anything and everything that promises a prize, I repeat that 'promises' a prize but after some time. And that is basically why we procrastinate.

When we know that we will have to wait after putting in the effort, our mind gives us stupid excuses to not work at all and then we waste our time.

This problem can be countered but again, you need the willpower to do so. You need the self-control and you must posses the energy required to bring about a big change. While we must continue to strive and not be greedy but we still love instant rewards. Set these instant rewards for yourself. Only give yourself a reward when you do something positive regarding your task. In order to do that, you must have a plan to achieve your goals. When you have a plan you know when you need to do what task. And when you know the tasks, you can set certain rewards for yourself after you are done with the tasks. Just like that, task by task, you will continue to make progress. Your rewards must be things which you normally take for granted. You can set watching your favorite TV show as a reward or getting a massage as one.

You can also discipline yourself by making yourself face short term consequences for not completing a task. You should have the courage to punish yourself by restraining yourself from doing things that you do for fun. Our minds take great actions when we put ourselves under pressure but it takes a lot of willpower to be able to do it. Not everyone can do it. If you have been following me from the start, you should understand the required toughness level of your mind and the willpower you need to do what I'm saying.

The most important thing is to do it regularly. If you fail to follow your own rules of rewards and punishments, your mind will know how weak you are and it won't give any heed to the rewards and punishments in future. Once you fail to commit to your rules, your mind will take over just like before and won't let you do anything except procrastination.

Another reason we procrastinate is that we don't have our priorities straight. We are confused about our own tasks. We sometimes can't decide what to do first and what to do next. It creates a storm in our mind and we end up doing nothing except wasting our time. If we know from the beginning that what our priorities are, it becomes much easier to follow the rules. When you know that a certain task is more important to you than any other task, you will always prefer to perform that task over anything else.

I can keep talking about it but the future is in your hands and you are the one who has to change it. You can either keep going like this and be a procrastinator all your life or you can start from today and change yourself for the better. It's never too late. All it takes a little consistent effort and then it becomes your habit. The hardwork seems hard only until you make it your habit. After that, it becomes your routine and you get adjusted to it.

In order to take action, you need a strong willpower and you must strengthen it by exercising your brain just like you would exercise your muscles.

When you have a motivation and the willpower to work hard for that motivation, you are less likely to procrastinate. You are more likely to push yourself under any kind of circumstances you face. It is more likely that you never sit back after a set back, instead you get back on your feet and say to the world, 'try me!'

One of the most successful ways to make yourself work harder is to talk to yourself. Gone are the days when people thought about talking to yourself as being crazy. No, you're not crazy for talking to yourself. You are absolutely okay. The thing is that no one else around you understands you like you understand yourself. You should not be shy of standing in front of the mirror, talking to yourself and giving yourself reaffirmations that you can do what you want to do.

CHAPTER 6

THE NEW SALVES

◆

Slavery is one of the darkest topics of our country. There are people today who would still love to have slaves just like their ancestors had them before it was officially abolished. With the abolishment of slavery, it's not possible to own a free man as a slave but what if I tell you that it still exists today? It exists in a new form, not like before. today's slaves are not Black only. They are from every race and the reality is that they choose to be the modern day slaves. Some without knowing and some while knowing. Some people get so deep into this swamp of modern day slavery that it becomes impossible for them to get out of it. People are still stepping into it every day and have a good chance of avoiding it and staying atop it. But it needs preparation. You can't cross a swamp by stepping into it. You need a boat and skills of driving a boat in order to cross it and stay away from it. And for that you must have the patience and willpower to do it.

The modern day slavery is not even illegal so you can't be saved because of government intervention. There isn't going to be another civil war to abolish this slavery because this slavery is not recognized as slavery. It is you and only you who can fight against this modern slavery. It's not that difficult if you possess the required energy and willpower and have a motivation to work for. When you have a motivation, you know where you want to end up. And when you have the willpower, you are able to actually end up where you want to be.

It's not possible to do it overnight so patience is the key to it. Let me explain to you how does this modern slavery exist. In today's corporate world, when you work for someone else, you are actually benefitting your boss. You get what is predefined salary for you with little increments and bonuses. It doesn't matter how hard you work, how much effort you put in, you never make the progress which you deserve. Your extra effort bears fruit for your boss only while you keep making the same amount of money. Your efforts don't directly affect your circumstances because after all, you are not working for yourself but for another man. What else is slavery in your point of view? I believe that this is what slavery is; working for another man without ever noticing your own abilities. You never realize what you could achieve if you started working for yourself. And that's because of the fears that this media and the people around you instill in your mind. They are always telling you the bad things that could happen if you take a bold step. All of this contributes to you thinking negatively. And when you think negatively, you start to lose hope. You can't believe in your own abilities. You lose faith in your own self. I've talked much about what negative thought do to you and your life in general. But I know how our minds work. They need to listen to the same things over and over again. It takes time to make your mind ready for a change.

I think it's better here to talk about the working of mind in order to make you understand how you can avoid being a slave. The first thing to do is to take control of your own mind. When you listen to the negative talks of the people around you for a long time, your mind integrates itself with the negative thoughts and you end up thinking negatively all the time. People are not your enemies, they are themselves afraid of what they are asking you to avoid. But the thing is that it's not beneficial for you. In order to get out of this circle, you need to stop giving heed to what people think and what people say.

The fear is a genuine thing. Whenever I think about the history of my fellow African Americans in this country, I get confused about it. You know, black people are generally much stronger than other races; it is natural and a gift from God. We must be thankful for it. The thing that confuses me the most is the fact that during the dark period when slavery was legal in this country, these my people would get enslaved in form of groups. They were forced to do labor without their will. They were beaten and were deprived of basic human rights. Their women would get raped. And still after all of this, they couldn't do a thing. They wouldn't revolt against the transgressors who made them work without pay. Why is that these men couldn't come together and fight against this brutality like my Haitian ancestors did to the French to gain their independence of Haiti 1804? That's because they were fearful for their lives and the lives of their loved ones. (Hence why Kanye said slavery was a choice) That's because their minds were filled with thoughts of being unsuccessful in their fight against slavery. Not even a single man wanted to be a slave but many lived their whole lives being slaves. This is what fear can do to you.

Now think about your own self. Are you not afraid of failure? Do you not think that you won't be able to make it through life if you stop working on your present job? Unfortunately, I know from personal experience that you are so fearful that you prefer living this life over a life full of freedom. The reason for this fear is the negative thoughts that fill your mind. These negative thoughts are what's not letting you make progress.

Let me share my own story here. Just like you, I always feared leaving my job. A part of me believed in myself that I could achieve what I wanted to but I was still fearful of failure. Back in those days, I was more failure conscious than success conscious. My negative thoughts ruled over my mind. I was a mediocre and felt comfortable being one. For 18 years I never bothered to take a bold step of doing something for my own self. I just wanted to live the day to day life because of my fears. I always had a desire of doing something for myself but my fears never let me do it.

After losing my job, I finally realized that I had no choice but to face my fears. I had to take those bold steps which I always hesitated to take. I needed to do something for myself in order to survive. Under immense amount of financial pressure I decided to start my own business. I sometimes think that I would have never done in had I not lost my job. I would have remained a mediocre my whole life while having just a desire and a dream to be my own owner. When I got pushed from the top of the cliff, I finally realized that I was making a big mistake until then.

It took me two years to get back on my feet and now I have two successful businesses running. The only reason I was able to accomplish my long time dream is that I finally took a step for my own future. I'm sure that had I not gotten fired, I'd never have been able to accomplish what I've accomplished now. I now regret the time that I wasted while serving and benefiting someone else. For sure, I learned a lot from that job but I'd have accumulated much more wealth had I chosen to start my own business earlier.

My questions here for you are simple and straightforward. For how long do you plan to serve and benefit someone else? And when are you going to take that one step which takes you ahead of everyone else? I hope you have the answers to these questions. If not, I hope and pray that you find your answers soon.

CHAPTER 7

LOVING YOURSELF

❖

If you have found the answers to my questions, you have actually done yourself a favor. You must understand that in your view the most important life in this world should yours. It's not called being selfish if you care about yourself and put yourself before everything else. Because for you the world exists only as long as you exist. If you stop caring about your own self, nothings matters for you after that. Caring about others is essential but loving your own self is much more important and should always be your first and utmost priority.

What would be your reply if I asked you if you love yourself or not? You'd definitely say yes but the reality might be different. You can't just say that you love yourself without actually doing it. Your actions speak louder than your words. So instead of asking yourself this question, look at your actions and decide if you love yourself or not. Look at the efforts and energy that you put in for others and the efforts and energy that you put in your own self. Now look at the results of these efforts. Are these results in your favor? Are you getting your fair share in return? Are people as much sincere with you as you are with them? Are you happy with all of the situations around yourself? These are just a few questions to ask yourself and you will definitely know whether or not you love yourself.

When you love yourself and care about yourself, you start to know your worth. Your self esteem increases in your own eyes and you start putting yourself first. You learn to say 'no' to people who are not worth your efforts. You start to decide what's good for yourself and what's not. You become the driver of your own life. You star to make your own choices. You are not bothered by what people care. You become your own focus and that is when you realize your true importance in people's lives. The people around you start to realize your efforts which they always took for granted.

Being successful doesn't mean working 24/7. In order to be successful you need to take care of yourself and work during designated hours only. Imagine how you would treat someone whom you love. Treat yourself the same way and you will realize what you were always lacking.

Appreciation gives everyone a big boost. When you are on a mission to achieve what seems difficult to achieve, appreciate your little achievements so that you keep getting the required boost. It will keep you going. It won't let you get tired. Try it with others; when you appreciate them, they start working with all honesty and effort. That's what appreciation does to you. You also deserve appreciation. Don't think of it like self-praise. That's a different thing. You appreciate yourself for a reason, for achieving something while self-praise doesn't have a base. It's done without any reason. Talk to yourself and give yourself a pat on the back. You absolutely deserve that.

When you appreciate your own self, you care less about people's appreciation. You become enough for yourself. Eventually you will notice a change in yourself. You won't need people's approval but approval from yourself. When you have reached that point in your life, just know that you have started to prioritize yourself and your decisions. This will give you the much needed confidence for achieving your goals. Understanding the fact that no one is perfect gives you the peace of mind. No one can be perfect because we are all humans. It's humanly impossible to not commit a mistake. What you need to do after making a mistake is to learn from it and try your best to never commit it again. Mistakes make you learn lessons that you'd have never been able to learn otherwise.

If you want to be happy with your progress, you must make peace with your past mistakes and also learn from them at the same time. If you keep feeling bad about your mistakes, you will not be able to learn from them; instead you would find yourself at constant rift with your own self. Stop blaming yourself for the mistakes. They happened for a reason so just forget and move on. Mistakes are a part of ourselves and we must own them in order to learn from them. You should be ready to make mistakes in future. You won't become perfect after working on yourself just a little bit. You need to keep improving yourself but never say that you are perfect.

Anyone who believes in themselves to be perfect always fails badly because they never take lessons from their mistakes since they never accept and own their mistakes.

Always believe in your abilities and never doubt yourself. That's how you boost your self confidence. If you lack self confidence, you are never able to perform even the smallest of tasks. Believing in yourself starts with believing in your abilities.

You must be thinking why I am talking about loving yourself here. The simple reason is that when you love yourself, you give most of your attention to your own needs. And when you give attention to your own needs, you realize that your efforts should be utilized more efficiently in order to better fulfill your needs. When you start thinking about your efforts, you start evaluating where your efforts are being utilized. It is only after this realization that you start focusing your efforts on the right things. Focus maximizes the results of your efforts and you start getting what you deserve. It is human nature that we are driven by the results of our efforts. When you get the desired results of your efforts, you get the boost that you need in order to keep going forward. You get the self confidence that is necessary to lead your own life and have an impact on the lives of other people around you. Being a leader begins with being content with your own self. If you are not happy with your own self, it won't be possible for you to lead anyone else into prosperity.

When you're not happy, you don't love yourself and think of yourself to be not capable of helping others. You think that if you can't improve your own life, how you could help and influence others. That is a tactic of the negative thoughts which fill your mind with pessimism. In order to influence someone else, the first thing you need is the peace of mind and the ability to be happy with your own self. Yes, it is actually an ability. You have to find ways to love yourself and be happy with whatever you achieve. As I discussed earlier, you have to love yourself by following a method. Being unhappy has become so common in today's modern age. Everyone is looking at the people ahead of them and not being happy. When you're not happy with yourself, you can't love yourself. Just like you won't love someone who doesn't make you happy. The key to loving yourself is to be happy with yourself first of all. When you are happy with yourself, it becomes much easier to love yourself.

You could be doing anything, even if you don't own a business; your productivity depends on how you treat yourself. If you treat yourself in the right way, success will come to you running. It's only possible to love yourself when you are happy with yourself. When you are happy with yourself, you appreciate yourself more and appreciation does a lot for you. Appreciation gives you the energy that you need. When you love yourself. you don't look at your mistakes and get upset, rather you try to improve yourself in order to not make mistakes in future. When you love yourself, you get to know your own abilities better. And then you are able to make use of these abilities and increase your productivity. When you love yourself, you start to develop the ability of becoming a leader. Only a person happy with himself can lead others; and that's possible only when you love yourself. The simple thing is to never look down upon your own self. That is one of the worst things to do and it always results in failure. You need to push yourself forward instead of backwards. That can be done by thinking positively about your achievements and being an optimist. When you are an optimist, you are actually always thinking positive and fill your thoughts with positivity. And as I've said earlier, your thoughts become your destiny.

 The time is right now. You will always have an excuse to delay your dreams of becoming independent and these dreams can only be accomplished right now. I urge you to not waste anymore of your time. Get up and "Just do it.

CHAPTER 8

AVOIDING NEGATIVE PEOPLE

❖

When you talk about success, things are not always easy for you. When you talk about ideas, not everyone thinks that your idea is worth working for. This is natural and you can't change that. But you can change one thing, and that is your behavior towards such people. You will find people who genuinely care about you and don't want you to fail. But there is no lack of people who will try to pull you down just because they don't want to see you be successful. This second kind of people is the hardest to deal with. You can never convince them and should never try to. The simple way of keeping yourself safe from their negativity is to avoid them.

I'd first like to talk about the people who genuinely care about you and don't want you to end up in a bad situation. When they see you working towards a bigger goal, they tell you about failure and warn you to not get into trouble. They don't want you to get hurt and waste your money. They are actually mediocre and want the same for you. They do it out of their own fear. They are incapable of taking control of their own minds. They can't take a bold step themselves so they don't want to you to take any step either. I do blame them for their weaker mentality which makes them fearful.

but after all, they are sincere with you. They don't want anything bad happen to you. They are not jealous of you. They just can't see the future you see. And hence they are ultimately negative for you. We don't need to care about people's sincerity; rather we need to look at their words because their words affect us the most. If they are talking about negative things and are instilling negative thoughts in your mind, they are simply not beneficial for you. When you need to take control of your thoughts, you can't allow such people to get into your mind and fill it with garbage and negative thoughts.

The way to deal with such people is to talk to them and evaluate why they think negatively and why they don't believe that you will become successful. You can notice from their answers that they are only fearful of failure and nothing else. They will only talk about what ifs. They won't talk about success at all. They will only warn you of failure. You can try to tell them that success also exists in this world and it only comes to those who strive and take action. If they understand your point then it's well and good. If they don't, you should simply not try to convince them anymore. You should not waste your energy on such people who are incapable of understanding your way of thinking and who are too fearful of failure that they can't take any action in order to change their own conditions. It is not your duty to convince people to support your ideas and you should not try to convince people beyond a certain limit. When you feel someone is not at all getting it, stop trying to convince them. Their thoughts will not affect your success but your own thoughts will. So you need to protect your own thoughts in order to be successful. If you keep trying to convince such people, it is a high chance that you will get caught into their thoughts and negativity which will affect your own success in a bad way. Be polite with them since they are sincere with you, but don't get into too much contact with them. Try to avoid them as much as you can but not so much that they start to notice it and get hurt. You are not here to hurt people but to be successful. These people will become your good clients when you have a successful business.

    The other kind of people is the ones who want to pull you down. They simply don't want you to be successful. They don't want to go ahead of themselves. It's right to say that they are jealous from you. They will do everything to convince you to stop working towards your goals and don't take any action. They will try to make you fearful of failure. They will be the helpers of your failure conscious but only if you let them be. If you are a success conscious person and have the willpower to work towards your goals, it should not be easy for them to let you down. But the most important thing to notice here is that they are like professionals. They are like serial killers of dreams. They are experienced at it and know how to pull people down. That's when things seem to start getting out of your hand. You might start giving in to such people's negative thoughts. And that's also when your hard work and your brain training come in handy. If you have trained yourself well, there are more chances that you won't allow them to fill your mind with negativity. If you have already won the battle of your own mind, it will be easier for you to ward off such thoughts and avoid such people.

These people don't only scare you with failure but they have their own tactics to stop you and convince you to quit. They will ask you to solve their problems and will try to waste your time. Remember that you are not anyone's problem solver especially when you know that there is a corrupt intention behind all of this. You should have the guts to say 'no' to such people and not let them waste your time. They will try to praise you for no reason in order to make you think big of yourself and make you work for them. You should be able to take charge of the conversation whenever you have one with them. You can only try to avoid them but they are on a mission so they won't let you avoid themselves. Now the only option for you is to make them talk about things of your choice. Don't share your ideas with them. Try to keep it a secret from them. All they are going to do is laugh at your idea and make fun of you. After all, they are deliberately trying to pull you down. In case they make you frustrated and try to get under your skin, don't become angry with them and don't be frustrated. You will only waste your own energy which should be used at something of your benefit. They will also taunt you for your short temper and will tell you that you can't achieve your goals with this temper. This will make you think like they are right and you will reconsider your plans. Never do that. There's nothing wrong in getting angry with stupid people who try to let you down. You are normal and should keep moving forward towards your goals.

One thing to always take care of is your thoughts. You should have the ability to always think positive and never let anyone fill your mind with negativity. What's good after all this grind if you let someone take control of your thoughts? It's normal to feel down for some time after a rough experience but you should have the willpower and the energy to get back up and keep doing what you are doing. I was fortunate enough to have the first kind of people during my own journey. These people are my friends and family. They were always sincere with me but they couldn't believe in me when I first shared the idea of starting a not-for-profit and a music organization. I had to learn everything by myself. These people laughed at me, made fun of me and told me that I'd fail. But they never actually wanted me to fail. I had to keep myself away from them for some time. Once I was near my goals, these same people actually started motivating me and they are still my motivation to this day. I am thankful to them for making me who I am today. Their doubts have made me stronger. Now that I've achieved what I wanted to achieve, these people praise me for my efforts and we are like a family.

    I'm sure that you will have the same outcome if you keep steadfast and don't listen to the negativity thrown at you by the people. It's just a matter of time that you will prove all these people wrong and will come out successful. All you have to do is stay strong.

CHAPTER 9

RETRAINING THE MIND

❖

When I talk about something, it might seem easy here. In reality, it's the opposite. It's not so easy to change your own mind. It's not that easy to forget all the negative aspects of anything and think about the positives only. That is how we are built. We are sometimes just not able to take control of our minds. We need to give attention to small things constantly in order to keep going.

Things get much more difficult during and after meeting people with negative thoughts. And unfortunately most of the people around us are not so positive for us. They pull us down, intentionally or unintentionally. The effects on us are pretty much the same. Some don't want us to take action because they care about us while others don't want us to take action because they don't want to see us succeed. We are not affected by their intention but their words. Doesn't matter how much we try to distance ourselves from such people, they somehow have an effect on us. They continue to let us down and it is usually us fighting against a whole lot of people. Sometimes you feel so down that you just want to quit. You get caught up in the negativity which you receive from the people around you. You get caught up in the fears that they introduce you to.

Believe me, there is going to be a point in your journey where you hit your bottom and your worst. You will just want to let everything go away so that you can have peace of mind. You will remember about all the hard work and sacrifices and will think that all of that is going to waste now. You think about all the late night hours and early mornings. You think about all the plans, goals and motivations that kept you going through all this time. You start thinking like it was a mistake that you set on this journey.

If you believe me then let me tell you that it's not the time to quit rather it's time to give your energy another boost. It's time to fight another battle of your mind and it's time to retrain your mind. That's the only way to get out of this situation. You need to know that it's not your own thoughts that are making you think about quitting. It's the other peoples' thoughts which are filled with negativity. These are the thoughts of the people who are afraid of taking even a single step. They can only praise you after you have accomplished something. They do not have the guts to start something from scratch because they are too afraid of failure. These are the thoughts of people who are failure conscious, not success conscious.

You should remember the time when you fought your first battle. The time before you started out for this new journey. You know you won that battle so you can win this battle again. You need to go back to your starting point in order to retrain your mind like the way you did it for the first time. Remember how you defeated your own negative thoughts. This time it's peoples' negative thoughts and hence it should be easy to defeat them.

If you have actually trained your mind before and have defeated the negative thoughts, you have actually established an immune system against negativity in your brain. It's going to be much easier now to fight against these thoughts.

You need to think again about why you began your journey. Think about your motivation and your goals. I believe if you have come this far, you have the willpower to keep going. It's just a phase of being overwhelmed by the negative thoughts and it will be over. The negative don't possess the energy that your mind possesses and it should be easy for you to get these out of your mind.

The worst thought is the thought of ending up as a failure. It simply jams your mind and doesn't let you work at all. When you are afraid of failure, you simply can't focus on your work since you have made it up in your mind that you are going to fail anyway, so why bother to work so hard. When you stop working, you actually fail at the end. The way to stop being fearful of failure is to think about the positive aspects of your plans and give them some time. Promise yourself to just think about the positives for a while. I'm sure that you will feel much better after a few such sessions of self therapy.

The other thing negative thoughts do to you is that they make you worried about your future. All of a sudden you start to think what will happen if this happens or what will happen if that happens. This is all lie and deceit. All you need to do is stay calm and not worry about what will happen. No one owns the future. You don't own it, I don't own it, and nobody in the world owns it. Future is owned by those you put in the effort. It is a natural law that if you keep going and keep striving, there is not 1% chance that you will not succeed. You are going to be successful at every cost. Look around yourself and find the people who became successful. They didn't become successful overnight. They worked hard for decades in order to become what they wanted to become. Our problem is that we want everything quickly and that's what makes most of the people unsuccessful. When people don't get the desired results in short time, they stop working towards their goals and give up on their dreams. You don't have to be and should not be one of these people. You should know that if you keep going, your time will come and you will succeed. The only thing that you need to do is keep going, have patience and never settle for less; never settle for mediocrity, instead settle the mediocrity.

CHAPTER 10

MONEY CAN BUY YOU HAPPINESS

❖

Money is a blessing and a curse at the same time. It is what you make it. If you use it purposefully, it becomes a blessing for you. If you use it for wrong purposes, it becomes a curse. We are all after money and want to earn it in order to live our lives peacefully. It is a blessing only as long as we keep it and spend it like a blessing. And it becomes a curse when it's wasted instead of being used.

Money is an important factor in our lives. It would be right to say that it has become the center of our worldly lives. We all strive to earn more and more money. Sometimes we even become greedy for it. I believe greed can be a good motivation for earning money but this motivation has to be controlled, otherwise it becomes a problem for you and the people around you.

Let's talk about both aspects of money here so that you know what you are going after. It's your decisions and morality that makes it either a blessing or a curse.

When you have money, things tend to get a little easier for you. You are

able to provide for yourself and your family. That's the basic purpose of
earning money. But there are other things to life in this modern world. Our needs have expanded just the world has expanded for us. You hear about the old times stories of how people used to live and can't imagine living that life. The simple life that seems to be a life without any worries. When people only needed food to eat, clothes to wear and a shelter over their head. That life seems impossible in today's world. If you have heard about the Amish people, you will have an idea about that life but the truth is that they are living the life which was called modern in 19th and 20th century. They are not living is stone age and have access to many modern things and occasionally use them.

With the expansion of technology, it has become a necessity for everyone to live a life up to the modern standards. It's not the food, clothes and shelter anymore that we require. It's a lot of other things that we need in our lives to live happily. And when you have people around you who enjoy the luxuries of life, you feel left behind. The internet and social media has made it more essential to get the luxuries in order to not feel left behind.

The big question we always ask ourselves is; can money buy happiness?
If you were lucky to be born in a nice and safe environment, with happy people around, you are most likely to be happy and have a content life.

When you have everything you need and can get what you want, is there anything stopping you from being happy? You must have heard the phrase;

money can't buy happiness, but have you ever actually pondered over it, or have you ever questioned this phrase?

Why can't money buy happiness? WHY NOT? The matter of fact is that MONEY CAN BUY YOU HAPPINESS! It all depends on how you see and perceive things.

Money can buy you happiness only if you spend it in the right way.

Remember, piling up money in a room doesn't make you rich, it makes you miserable. You earn money to spend it on things which make you happy. That's how you buy happiness with money. If your sole purpose is to pile up money without any idea to spend it, then the money is useless

When you spend money on experiences, it gives you relief, peace of mind and a satisfaction you'll rarely feel if you never had that experience.

Let's take an example. If you buy a very costly phone, it will stay with you

for the coming months or may be years. But if you spend that same amount of money on a vacation, the vacation will be over in the next few days but it will make you much happier than buying a costly phone. I'm not saying that buying a costly phone doesn't make you happy. But it's the experiences

that make you comparably happier. The experience itself will not stay with you but the memory will. And whenever you think of that memory, it will make you happy. We see the distant things as more pleasing. The vacation

which is now over, still makes you happy because you long for another such vacation. And that's how it makes you happier than buying materials.

Materials on the other hand give you a lot of comfort. A comfortable car is definitely a better ride but you can only buy it with money. A costly smart phone surely makes it easier for you to work. It saves you time and energy.

You're never stressed. The absence of stress from your life should make you happy. A better car is good enough just for the looks. People keep praising it for how good it is. That always makes you happy. And the bonus is the comfortable ride which doesn't result in the back ache. A beautiful and furnished house will always make you happy. A house with all the necessities of life you want is better than anything. You come back from work to a beautiful place you actually love to live in. That's what makes you
 happy.
When you have money, you can spend it on people you love. You can take your wife to the best restaurants in the city. Her happiness will definitely make you happy. You can send your children to the best school in the town for a better future. You don't have to worry about sending them to
 university. You can afford any university they choose to attend. You don't have to tell them that you can't buy them something, can't take them
    somewhere or can't give them what they want when you have money. Even the thought of all of this is so good. You don't have to worry about anything when you have the money.
When you have enough money, you don't have to worry about the debts. You don't need to worry about paying bills. You don't have to worry about
 buying a gift for a loved one's birthday. You don't have to worry about an unexpected expense. Financial stress is the most lethal kind of stress and it can lead to very harmful results. You can be stress free all the time. You can avoid all the tensions which people experience due to lack of money. Shouldn't that make you happy?

While going through a tough phase in a relationship, you can easily say good bye to the things causing problems by packing you bags, going for a
 vacation and coming back to a happy relationship.
When you are rich, people want to be around you. They don't necessarily need anything from you but your attention. They like to talk to you and be friends with you so that they can let the world know about their rich friends
 and connections. Poverty leads to poor social connections as you go out less and stay where you are. If you don't have the money to go out with friends, they will soon forget you and find new people to hang out with.

    When you go at places where wealthy people go dinning and travel in the business class, you come in contact with wealthy people. Their experiences help you in sorting out your own problems. You can not only become their friend but also learn a lot from them.
When you are rich, you can buy what you like. You don't have to restrict
 yourself because of the low budget. You don't have to wait until the next month to buy something which you want to buy now. You don't have to closely manage the budget in order to make room for certain things you want to buy.
The thought of being financially stress free is energizing enough to make you work for the money you deserve.
It is a human instinct that we get comfort and satisfaction when give back to
 the community. We all have heard it and have seen the wealthy do it. They give back to the community because they know the hardships they've faced. They want the younger generation to have better circumstances so that they can grow into successful people. Helping others definitely makes

you happy. It makes you happy to be able to have an influence over someone's life. When someone depends on you for their needs to be fulfilled, you feel the strength. You play a role in changing someone's life.

They stay humble towards you. They are always thankful to you. They remember you in good and kind words. They praise you publically and privately. Shouldn't that make you happy?

Another way of buying happiness with money is to help a loved one. Helping a sibling, a relative or a friend in need gives you the utmost
 satisfaction and peace of mind. You don't even have to think twice before lending a helping hand. You can throw a birthday party for a loved one without a problem. You can do what you want to do and can get what you want to get. Money has the power to get you whatever you want.

Money can also buy you a lot of free time. There must be things which you don't like to do yourself and would rather spend the time doing something else. You can pay others to do the chores for you and use the time to make
 more money than you spend on the workers.

If you're a history lover, you can collect antiques. If you're an art lover, you can collect paintings. If you're a sports lover, you can go and watch the games live. If you're a car lover, you can buy the car you can only dream
 of. By paying off your mortgage, you gain the choice of working part-time, or
having a longer holiday. By putting money aside for your children's future, you gain the choice of where they might go to school, or which extracurricular activities they might take part in. By having savings rather than debt you reduce stress in relationships; often an enormous contributor to happiness.

Money won't make you happy in isolation. As an illustration, we often see successful artists who earn huge amounts of money succumb to drug addiction. Money in this case is perhaps the enabler of self-destructive behavior.

In short, money can buy you happiness if you want to. If you use your money properly, there's no one stopping you from buying your happiness with the money you have. The world has more poor people than rich

 people. The majority does believe that money can't buy you happiness and that money is evil.

Money can buy you happiness. But only if you choose to buy happiness with it.

CHAPTER 11

❖

FINDING YOUR PURPOSE

Most of us have a natural will to achieve what we don't have. Not having something is actually what makes you want something. Make sure what you don't have and want to have. It helps you to focus on your problems and then solve them accordingly.

Why do you want something is the most important question. If you're confused about this "why", then you need to work on it first. If the reason is indeterminate or unclear, then your motivational energy will be the same. While motivation gives you energy to do something, that energy needs to be focused on something specific. So without meaning, there is no direction for your energy to be focused on.

So why not take some time today and think about where you're right now? Take one part of your life that you'd like to be changed.

For example, it may be your current job. First, start with 'why'. Write down your reasons for why you're in the job in the first place. Then think about your Purpose. Write down what it is within your job that gives you meaning, what are the things that you don't like about it, and what are some things that will help push you forward in life.

If you want to start a business then think about your 'why'. Why do you want to start this business? I know you have a motivation but that is not essentially your 'why'. The basic reason for starting a business is to earn money. But the question here is that why do you want to earn that money? What is it that you need in your life which you can have after earning the money?

Finding your purpose is the base of doing anything in your life. If you want to provide a better life to yourself and your family, that is your purpose. If you want to financially help people around yourself, that is your purpose. If you want to earn money to life a better life after retirement, then that is your purpose. Whatever it is, you must have a purpose in order to make yourself work harder. Motivation and purpose are slightly different and should not be confused. Motivation gives you the energy to work and your purpose is what makes you work actually. A life without purpose is not worth living.

You can't live a life without purpose. You will be left far behind if you don't choose a purpose of your life.
When you have a purpose, you have a reason to work for. You are not shooting in the dark; instead you have a point to target. When you shoot in the dark, you actually harm others and also your own self. When you have a point to target, you

don't only save your energy and your time but also become successful. Life is just like that; you can only be successful if you have a purpose to live by. In addition to having a purpose, you should be able to do anything in order to achieve that purpose. You should have the willpower and the energy to work towards that purpose. In order to have the willpower and energy, you need to have the mind that can produce that willpower and energy. It is you and only you who can do all of this for yourself. No one else will work for you if you are not willing to work for yourself.
Everything comes back to the same point which I've talked about all along. First of all, you need to settle and let go off the thought of being a mediocre. Then you should be able to win the battle of your own mind and think about the positives all the time. You need to have a motivation and a purpose. It is only then that you will succeed in getting what you want to get. And the keys to success are patience and consistency; you can only get these keys by constant practice.
My purpose of writing this book was to share my own experience with you. I wanted to help you by letting you know the things that I needed in my own journey. I was not alone in my journey; I had the help of my mentors whom I am

thankful to till this day. I had to seek help from many people. I've compiled all of the knowledge that I gained so that you can take benefit from it too.

I hope that you realize your own capabilities and start doing something from today. If you keep waiting for a perfect time, it won't ever come. Your time is now and you must start working today, not tomorrow but today and right now! I wish you good in your future endeavors and I hope that you will finally succeed after training your mind and working constantly while being patient.

Made in the USA
Middletown, DE
11 April 2023